My Life with Dea

An Unexpected Love Story

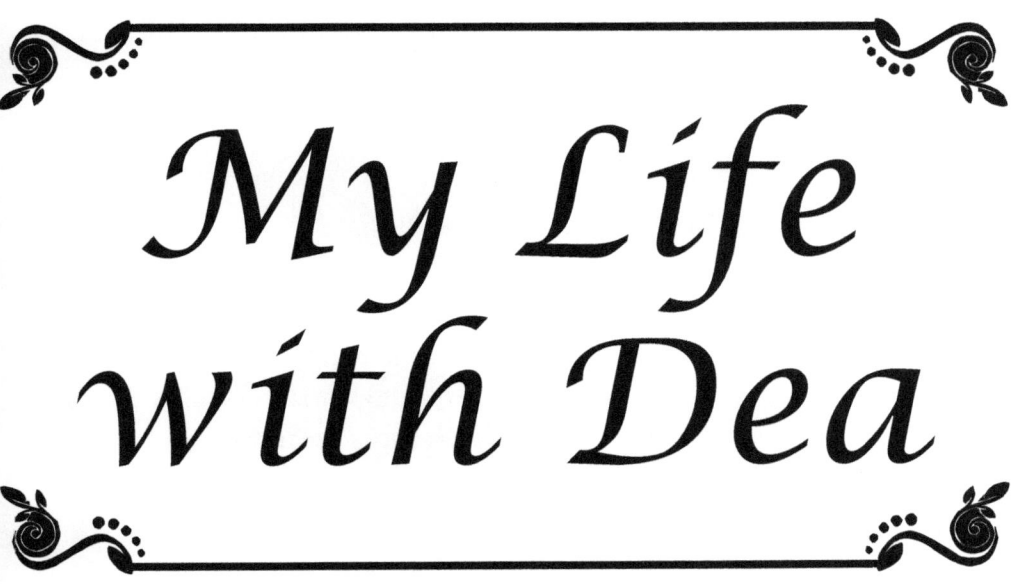

My Life with Dea

An Unexpected Love Story

Patrick Wade

Edited by Tabitha Kerr

CITI OF
BOOKS

CITIOFBOOKS, INC.
3736 Eubank NE Suite A1
Albuquerque, NM 87111-3579
www.citiofbooks.com

Hotline : 1 (877) 389-2759
Fax :   1 (505) 930-7244

Ordering Information:

Quantity sales. Special discounts are available on quantity purchases by corporations, associations, and others. For details, contact the publisher at the address above.

Printed in the United States of America.

ISBN-13:   Paperback   979-8-89391-881-6
           eBook   979-8-89391-882-3

Library of Congress Control Number: 2025917712

In memory of my wife, Dearest Clayton-Wade, who has given me much love and joy over the years.

Contents

My Wife i

Introduction iii

Chapter 1 : My Job and the Move to a New Town 1

Chapter 2 : The Dating Game and Meeting My Soulmate . . . 8

Chapter 3 : The Day We Got Married 14

Chapter 4 : The Big Move Back to St. Louis 18

Chapter 5 : An Overseas Assignment 22

Chapter 6 : The Big Move Back Home 28

Chapter 7 : The Final Days 31

About the Author. 35

MY WIFE

My wife, my joy, my happiness!
You are the substance by which my soul exists.
How do I love you?
Let me number the ways—
But there doesn't exist a number high enough.
Let me express in words—
But there isn't a word that can elucidate how I feel.
Let me show how much I care—
But what deed can I do that will show just how I feel.
No matter what action I take, it could never have
the excitement or enthusiasm that can exemplify my love.
So I must revert to the most simple form of all.
For in simplicity lies complexity.
By stating just three simple words, can I truly count,
express, and show just how much I feel.
Here then is the most complex form of my love.
Simply put, I Love You!

April 20, 1992

INTRODUCTION

This book is a story about a wonderful journey in becoming a field service engineer, moving to a new town, meeting the most wonderful person of my life, and the adventures we had together over the years. After all, every love story has its beginning, middle, and end. So goes this novelette as this is based on a true love story with all its ups and downs and how I managed to have a wonderful journey with a person to whom I never expected to find in a town that I never expected to go.

CHAPTER 1

My Job and the Move to a New Town

Be it fate or divine intervention or making the right decision at the right time, my life was about to change forever. They say things happen for a reason, and I would not be here if I hadn't been there. We are given a lot of choices along the way, and it's these choices that will get us to where we are supposed to be. You never know what will happen, and so we must be prepared to change when the opportunity comes along.

To start my journey, I must go back to where my life took an unexpected turn, and I must ask the question, Is life predestined by fate, and do we have no control over it? No matter what forces were involved, I had a wonderful adventure and loved every minute of it.

Let me first explain my job and how I became a field service engineer. You see, it all started when I quit the US Air Force in late December of 1980 with an honorable discharge to work with this company, which was based in St. Louis, as an automatic test equipment (ATE) engineer. I already had my BS degree in EET (electronic engineering and technology) and AS in computer science, and thus the company hired me as an ATE engineer to work on this very stressful project, which I had worked on while in the air force. The pay was good, and I managed to find a nice place to live in St. Louis.

The company was in the process of updating the project and hired me to work on designing some test equipment. At first, the job was great, and it was fun in designing new test equipment.

Imagine me, a successful engineer. Growing up I never thought I would become an ATE engineer, working on a very important project. I started out in college as a mathematician, then wind up changing my degree to engineering and technology degree and now working at a company designing some test equipment.

As the days went by, the working hours became longer, and having a deadline to finish the design was becoming very stressful. Then my boss at that time told me that there was an opening in the Field Service Department as a field service engineer. He felt that this position would best suit my talents and skills. The job was on the same equipment I presently was working on as an engineer, but it meant me going out into the field to support the upgrade. It meant me going back to some of the bases and see some of the airmen that I once worked alongside when I was in the air force. Plus, it seemed to be the next logical step going forward in advancing my career.

However, before I made this big move into field service, I had to talk it over with my wife at the time as this would affect both of us and our daughter Sarah. I thought I married a wonderful person who would support me, and we could do many things together. After all, this would be a great opportunity for me, and I could make more money in hopes of getting a long-term assignment. Plus, maybe we could do some traveling together, and my daughter who was nine years old could see more of the county.

I adored Sarah and just wanted to make her life and her mother's life a little more enjoyable. However, in the beginning, it meant being on the road without them from time to time since I was at the bottom of the totem pole sort to speak. The company didn't pay for wives and their family to be with them while on short assignment.

With my wife's blessings, I switch jobs from an ATE engineer to the field service engineer and took off on several short-term contracts in various cities, helping out with the support equipment, which my company sold to the military. Even though my wife agreed for me to change jobs from ATE engineer to field service engineer, I could see that she began to regret it. I tried to assure her that I would be able to come home from time to time to be with her, but she still did not see the light at the end of the tunnel sort to speak. I tried to explain to her that there could be a long-term assignment coming up soon, but it will come a little later after I make these short trips.

But beyond my control, it seems that her mother played a bigger role in this situation, and thus my wife could not take it any longer and wanted to go home. As to why, well, that is for another story. Was fate playing a role here, or did I make a bad decision of getting into field service? No matter the reason, life forces have been put into motion, and my life was about to change.

On my last short assignment in early 1984, when I came home, I came home to an empty house. You see, while I was out on my last short assignment, when my wife called up her bother and he came out and got her and my daughter, Sarah and moved them all back to New Mexico.

Well, now things began to unravel, and unbeknownst to me, this change was about to change my life for a much greater adventure then I could have imagined.

A few days later after my wife left, I was wondering what to do next. I got a letter from her, stating that she wanted a divorce.

What a "dear John" letter. Not just a letter asking me to give her a divorce but that she could not live with me being on the road most of time.

Wow, now what do I do? Should I quit the company and move out west to be with her or grant her the divorce and move forward with my life? I didn't want to lose my job because it was a good-paying job, and I could see good things happening with this company. Plus, I wasn't sure of getting a new job out west. There were some job opportunities, but they require a full engineering degree, and I only had an engineer and technology degree.

I tried to explain to her on how things work. I told her that I could land a long-term contract soon, but she would not hear of it and wanted out. I fear that her mother had put ideas into her head, and so she just wanted out.

Here I was in a big town alone, trying to make the biggest decision of my life, and just not sure what to do or where life would take me.

I informed some of my friends and coworkers about what was happening, and they tried to console me, but still coming home to an empty house was a bit sad as I tried to keep a marriage together.

You see, marriage should last forever, and I really didn't want to get a divorce, but at the same time, I am not going to force someone to stay with me if they don't love me. One has to love someone of their own free will, and if they don't love you anymore, then it wasn't meant to be, and one should move forward. After all, you should not force anyone to stay if they are unhappy; it just makes everyone more miserable.

While my life was changing and not knowing where it would take me, I managed to get a long-term contract in house with the company base in St. Louis. I would stay in St. Louis for the most part and try to solve problems by phone if at all possible, and of course, I would have to travel to the bases if I could not solve the problems by phone. For the most part, I would be in one location for at least one year and maybe longer.

If only she could have waited a couple of more months, I would have been able to stay home with her 90 percent of the time, but now things had changed. Not wanting to quit my job, I started the procedure of getting the divorce like she wanted.

So my wife has now became my ex.

I didn't want to explain the reason as to why we split up to my fellow coworkers and friends I just wanted to get the heck out of Dodge or, in this case, out of St. Louis, where my company was based and where my soon-to-be ex and I lived for the past three plus years. At the present time, there doesn't seemed to be any long-term contract for me to go to because of two reasons: for one, I was already on a one-year-long contract; second, there was no one I could swap with as that was the only way for me to move outside of St. Louis. With that in mind, I began to settle down, thinking that I would be staying in St. Louis for at least a year or more. I proceeded with the divorce, and I started the process of buying a new car since my old car was slowly falling apart. This was in late February of 1984, and everything seemed to be going along fairly well until my new boss came to me and asked me if I wanted to move to Warner Robins, Georgia.

Well, it only took me a second to answer, and I stated, "Sure, I will go."

I did not want to spend any more time than possible in St. Louis, even though my divorce had begun, and I had signed a contract of buying a new car. My boss told me that he would get back to me later that day. Well, it was in March 1984 that he came back to me with an offer.

You see, I was already on a contract, which was based in St. Louis as mentioned, helping the military throughout several bases that had problems with the support equipment. My boss again made it clear that I didn't have to take the assignment, but that I could swap contract with another field service engineer who was on a long-term contract at Warner Robins, Georgia, and needed to move back to St. Louis.

So here comes the big question, Do I swap now or wait until later because I was already in the middle of a divorce and trying to buy a new car? I thought about it and made the decision to accept the offer of going to Warner Robins because I could always come back to St. Louis to finish filing for my divorce and buying my new car.

I told my boss, "Sure, I would go," and he said he'll make things happen. A couple of days later, the contract swapped was approved, and I would be on my way to Warner Robins within a few days.

I had to wait until all the details were made before I could make the move to Warner Robins. Since I had signed a contract with the dealership in buying a new car and I was going to use my old car as trade in, I didn't want to have to drive my old car all the way to Georgia and back. So before I left for Warner Robins, I went to the dealership and gave them my old car and then proceed to get ready to fly to Warner Robins.

The dealership had assured me that my new car would be ready in a couple of weeks. With the divorce in progress, I was hoping to come back and finish the divorce and pick up my new car all at same time.

My boss came back to me and with all the details of going to Warner Robins, Georgia. At age of thirty-four years old and on the verge of being divorced, plus waiting for my brandnew car to be delivered, I agreed to leave right away.

I was now off to Warner Robins, Georgia, on my first long-term assignment in mid-March 1984. Granted I had hope to still be married and watch my daughter grow up in a new, town but over the next few months, what was about to happen would change my life for a very long time.

When I got to Warner Robins, I met with the field service engineer to whom I was replacing. He was renting a nice house, and he asked me if I wanted to take over his lease. Since I really didn't want to have to go looking for a furnish place to live, I agreed. After all, his place was fully furnished, and it was in a great area.

You see, I didn't have any furniture of my own. In fact, all I own could fit into one very large box. Now that I had a house to live in, all I need was to get my new car and complete my divorce. The next step was in calling the car dealer, which I did several times to find out when my car would be ready. All they stated was soon, and that it was next in line to be built.

My lawyer called me and told me that my divorce was on the docket, and I needed to come up to sign the final divorce decree.

I then called the dealership up and told them that I was coming back to St. Louis within two days, and they had better have either my old car or my new car. Well, I knew that they didn't have my old car as it was long gone. They offer me a new car similar to the one I ordered before leaving St. Louis, but with a lot of extra stuff, which I really didn't care to have. However, I told them that I would agree in sharing half the increase price, and I will pick up the car within two days. They agreed to the new terms, and thus I would have a much fancier new car.

Once I arrived back in St. Louis, I finalize the divorce and then pick up my new car, a 1984 Dodge Dayton turbo. This was in mid-April of 1984, and once everything was signed, I drove back to Warner Robins, Georgia, to begin my new assignment.

As I mentioned, I took over leasing the house from my fellow field service engineer whom I was replacing, but I had to sign a new lease with the landlord. It seems that the new landlords were nice people, and while we were going over the house and making sure everything was okay for me to sign the new lease, they informed me about several things to do in town.

Being single, they told me about where I can meet new people. They mentioned that the town had a bowling alley, a typical movie theater, and another theatre that does live plays. They mentioned that the live theatre was a very good place to meet new people along with the bowling alley.

Now that I was settling into a nice house and began working on my new assignment, things began looking pretty good. In fact, this town was the beginning of my new life adventure.

CHAPTER 2

The Dating Game and Meeting My Soulmate

I'm not the one who likes being single, but here I am single with time on my hands. I really need to go out and do things in order to meet people of the opposite sex like getting involve with some kind of activity to where I can meet a nice lady who likes the same things that I like.

First, I thought I would go bowling and join a couple's team, even though I was only one half of a couple, but there are usually teams that need a fourth player.

The bowling was within walking distances from my house, and that made it easier to go and check to see about joining a league. The bowling leagues where all about to finish for the season, but they told me that I could come back later in the summer, and maybe there would be some summer leagues, which I could join. Well, I did do that, but in the meantime, while I was there, I went and bowled several games to try and keep my average up until the leagues started later in the fall.

Secondly, I thought why not give the live theatre a try since I had done some plays in my time, one in grade school, again during my senior year of high school, and once more when I was in college. Granted they were not big roles, but nevertheless I did enjoy doing live acting.

Looking back, at my first play called *Be Home before Midnight.* This play was about a family where there was a mother, father, and three children. I played the oldest son, then there was a middle daughter, and finally the youngest son. In the play, I tried to sneak home before midnight (hence, the title of the play), but it was 1:00 a.m.

As I entered the house, the clock struck 1:00 a.m., but with my bright idea, I decided to move the clock's big hand back to midnight, which meant that it chimed thirteen times.

That was when the mother got up, noticing that she had heard the clock striking thirteen times as she looked around, and that was when she spotted me, trying to hide. This was when the fun begins. The father was awoken to discussion between the mother and me. He came down to see what was going on when he spotted us talking about being home before midnight and to be more like my little brother, as if he was an angel. Then the daughter walked in, and so now they got on to her about being home before midnight and, of course, to be more like our younger brother.

Here is the ironic ending, guess who came in next—you guessed it—it was our younger brother.

So I figure, Why not give it a try and have some fun? I went to check out the local live theatre called Warner Robins Little Theatre or WRLT for short. It just so happened that they were having an audition for an upcoming play called *Visit to a Small Planet*. I went down to the local WRLT and met several nice people and audition for the play. I did not dream that I would get a part. I mean I was very nervous, and I have a really hard time in meeting new people since I was a bit shy. Plus, getting up in front of strangers was also a bit scary. I read for a part of an alien who comes back to earth to get his son who was raising havoc on earth. After my reading, I sat around while other people read for various other characters.

Once the audition was over, I just came back home to my house and waited for the call back.

Work got busy since I took over the job from the prior field service engineer. I just wanted to get settle in for a good long contract of hopefully five years or more. The town was medium-size about fifty thousand people, not too small but defiantly not too large. I would say just about right to get to know people or run into people on a more constant bases than being in a very large town. However, in a small town, you would run into the same people a lot more often, so I was glad that this town was about medium-size. Well somehow, I missed the first couple of call backs during the week as I didn't have an answering machine hooked up as yet.

When I did manage to hear from WRLT during the weekend and found out that I actually got the part of playing the alien if I wanted it, I was surprised, excited, and a bit nervous all at the same time. Of course, I said yes, and I would love to do the part.

It was Saturday when I went down to Warner Robins Little Theatre and began the rehearsal for my part in the play *A Visit to a Small Planet.* Here was where I met with several wonderful people who were playing several parts in the play as well as several crew members.

The young lady who did my makeup went by the name Dearest or Dea for short. Yes, that is correct: Dearest F. Clayton, such a pretty name and one I could not forget.

She had two teenage daughters Christinna (or Chris for short) and Michelle who help with the theatre from time to time. In fact, it was Chris on scrip, meaning that she followed along in the scrip to make sure the actors knew their lines in the play. Dea, who was doing my makeup, also helped with the set building. She asked me if I could help with building the set. I said not a problem as I was pretty good with a hammer and nails as they say.

This play was going to be my first play of many more while living here in Warner Robins. At first, I was a bit nervous in the fact that I didn't know anyone there, and I didn't know how to do my makeup, but Dea came to my rescue. She introduced me to the entire cast and crew, which help calmed me down. Plus, she said she would be with me throughout the play and made sure my makeup was put on just right for the play.

I slowly overcome my shyness as the rehearsal went along. Getting up in front of a crowd can be very scary, but the theatre was small, and that made it a bit easier.

The play was a success.

They say once you start acting, you will get the acting bug and want to do more, and thus my theatre days have begun, and it was a lot of fun.

Being single again, just meant that I could date anyone, and with doing these live plays, maybe I could find someone that had the same interest in doing things. I now started to enjoy life again, and the search to finding my true soulmate had begun.

As far as getting to know Dea, we just became friends at first and didn't do much dating in the beginning but did begin doing a lot of plays together. She became my personal makeup artist when I was acting. I also ran lights and sound and build sets and just became an all-around handyman. It was tough being single.

I started dating again to see what will happen and if I could find someone to be with for the rest of my life. Dea at the time didn't want to get serious at this point since I just got divorce and she wanted to make sure I was single for at least three years before getting really serious.

Anyway, like I have mentioned, I started dating but nothing was going well as usual. My cousin even tried to hook me up with a gal from Michigan, but since I lived in Georgia, that wasn't going to work well—no long-distance relationship does. Plus, at that time, my phone bills were getting pretty costly since we didn't have cell phone at that time. I finally let go of her as things weren't going anywhere.

Then I tried to date some local ladies, but again nothing really was happening, me being too short, too old, or just too something. Plus, I have always been shy when it comes to the ladies. Now being back on the dating scene, just wasn't getting me anywhere.

However, as fate would have it, Dea and I started to get closer as time went by. The more plays we did together, the closer we got.

Now here is the funny part during one of the plays, while we were performing, her two daughters were backstage outside the back door and watching their mother and I talk. They decided right then that I would make a great dad and a perfect husband for their mother.

As time went by, I got really involved in various plays like I mentioned. One such play was called *My Three Angels*. This play was about a store manager and his wife and their daughter. The owner of the store wasn't a very nice man, and so when the store owner came around to audit the books, things began to happen. Dea and I played husband and wife, and that was the funny part. We were not actually married, but a lot of people thought we were married because we played so well in the play as husband and wife. So that was pretty cool and again a lot of fun.

We were really getting close by now, and it was during one of the play's rehearsals of *My Three Angels* that we decided to take our relationship to the next level. She took my hand and led me to her boudoir. Like I said I'm a shy person and not the aggressor.

That was our first night of becoming more than just friends and what a night it was. Oh, I could have stayed the whole night until dawn, but alas, I had to go to work the next day and so somewhere around 1:00 or 2:00 a.m., I managed to go back to my house.

Now comes the aspect as to what to do next. Like I mentioned, she wanted to make sure that I was at least three years of being single, thus making sure I wasn't going back to my ex, as if that would ever happen. Plus, making sure that I was getting the dating scene out of my system and need to commit to one person.

As of this point, we had an open relationship of being able to date who I want as well as she could do the same. After all we were two consenting adults. Things got pretty interesting, and after a few more nights like this one, she finally asked me to move in with her and the kids. The kids like the idea of having a man around the house as it made for a bit safer since they lived in a trailer park.

It's funny how life goes. Just when you figure things out things change, and now you are on this new path, and where it goes is anyone's guess.

Dating wasn't really my thing as I wasn't very good at it. I have dated in the past (before I met my ex or Dea), and things never seemed to go well. Even though I knew how to treat a lady, it seems that the ladies that I have dated in the past wanted a guy with more aggressiveness. You know take the lead, but for me I wanted to make sure that they like me before getting involved. After all, I wasn't the most good-looking guy. You know the type, tall dark and handsome.

I try not to push a lady into something she doesn't want or like. My belief was that if you love someone, allow it to be free, and if she stays, then you know that she is the one.

Thus, it seems that my life will get even more interesting, and fate will once again wind up doing big things during the next few years. When Dea ask me to stay with her, things began to get very serious.

I believe that I finally met someone who I can truly love. In fact, I was falling in love with Dea more and more each day and with each play that we did together. Was this going to be my soulmate? Would her kids still like me after living together?

Well, I sure hope so because that means my dating game was over and I could see spending the rest of my life with her.

CHAPTER 3
The Day We Got Married

Dea and I were becoming very serious since the time I moved in with her. As mentioned, I moved down to Warner Robins in April of 1984, and now here it was March 1987, getting close to my three years of being divorce. Boy, how times flies, and now I have become a one-woman person again. We had done a lot of plays together and got involved with several theatre groups. We must have done about forty-four plays. Wow! That's a lot. We have done plays with Perry Players and Warner Robins Children Theatre (WRCT for short) and, of course, WRLT. I became president of WRCT for one year, plus I became VP of children theatre of the state of Georgia. It was a lot of work, but I loved it.

Ever since the play *My Three Angels,* Dea and I spent a lot of time together doing all kinds of plays together for the past three years. I even played Scrooge in *The Christmas Coral,* which was done by WRCT, and, boy, that was a lot of acting. We have built sets together, and I also ran lights and sound.

Dea managed to do some acting, best known for the play called *Tribute*, where she played a nurse. Like I mentioned, we had lots of fun doing these plays for the past three years. It was during the spring of 1987 that I was told that my contract may or may not get renewed.

With that in mind and the fact that since we were not married, Dea would not be able to come back with me to St. Louis. Well, it so happened that it has been three years when I met Dea and her daughters, Chris and Michelle, who now wanted to know just when we were getting married, what else could I do but to ask my beautiful lady to marry me? But it wasn't until the following night after we made love and were snuggled in each other's arms that I asked her to marry me, and of course, she said yes.

Now the problem was that if I was going to leave in October 1987, we need to get married before then. So the rush was on, as we needed to get married soon in case my contract didn't get renewed. Since there was a loll in doing the live plays, we had to come up with a date so that her brothers and their wives could attend and including our friends. I had to pick a best man, and she had to pick a maid of honor.

First came the date, and that was the twenty-fifth of May. Why this date? Well, it was halfway between our birthdays, and it was also Memorial weekend. At least we could not forget our anniversary. Ha! I pick Rick as my best man who was my friend, and we both work for the same company. Dea picked Christy from her work and who worked on several plays with us as well. Now all was set, well, sort of. We didn't have any church in mind really. I knew that she wanted to get married in a Catholic church, but we could not get our previous marriages annulled in the eyes of the Catholic church. So we went with my church, which was called the Reorganize Church of Latter-day Saints (not the Mormons from Utah but from Independence, Missouri).

My church had a little branch in Warner Robins, which made it great for us to get married. It was a small church and the perfect size for our wedding, plus, I knew the minister. Now that we had a church, a minister, a best man, and a maid of honor, what was left? Well, the girls Chris and Michelle wanted to be a part of this as well. Each had a boyfriend at the time. We said yes and all became part of the wedding party. I got Bill to sing for us, and all was fine. We even decided to have the reception in the house that we were living in at the time. So now everything was set. What could go wrong, right? Well, it was May 25, a Monday, being the last Monday of the month, and it was the official Memorial Holiday as well.

Everything looked perfect. I got ready and went to the church ahead of the bride to make sure everything was set up properly. I ushered the guest to their seats, made sure Bill was ready to sing, and the pianist was ready. In fact, she was playing some music while we all waited for the rest of the wedding party to arrive like my wife to be and her daughters. Then us guys, Chris's and Michelle's boyfriends, along with my soon to be father-in-law, all were waiting for girls to show up. As we waited, this was when I realized that she was always going to be late arriving at events, but this time she was extremely late due to having a bad hair day as they say and being very anxious. Her daughters were trying to help with her hair and keeping her calm at the same time. This made for some tense moments; however, I would have waited all day for her as I was deeply in love with her.

The funny part was her dad took me aside and told me that it wasn't too late to run. Ha! He did have a dry sense of humor.

I knew she loved me, and so I waited, and finally she arrived, and the ceremony began. First, I went up to the alter, and then Chris and Michelle with their boyfriends followed. Then finally the special moment, she came strolling down the aisle with her dad who gave her away. It was a nice simple wedding ceremony. Bill sang a couple of songs, and everyone stood up as she walked down the aisle, and then the minster began the ceremony, and within minutes we were married. The rest of the time went pretty well as we took a lot of pictures to have for our wedding album. We got to the house and change clothes, and then the guest arrived, and we had a nice reception. I could not believe that we were now man and wife, such a wonderful feeling.

Now that we were married, we had to go on a honeymoon. It was early fall, and we decided to go to Helen, Georgia, a nice quaint German town settled in the hills of upper Georgia. We enjoyed ourselves there and visited a lot of small shops. There was this Christmas shop that had lots of ornaments, and that's how we got started in collecting ornaments for our Christmas trees. While we were in Helen, Georgia, we also visit a little clock shop that got its cuckoo clocks from the Black Forest of Germany. Here was where a very interesting fact came into view. We had no idea in the world that one day, we would be going to Germany on an assignment for my company. Since we love cuckoo clocks, and I heard a lot about the Black Forest of Germany, we went ahead and bought a small one as that was all we could afford at the time. It was a pretty town, and we thought that maybe someday we would visit the Black Forest in Germany, but for now I was still on contract to stay in Warner Robins, Georgia. In fact, it was a couple of more years before my contract ended. But all good things must come to an end, and finally in October 1989, my contract didn't get renewed. Since my contract ended, I had to move back to St. Louis, and now my new family could accompany me back.

We had a lot of fun living as one (husband and wife) and doing various plays. I would like to mention all the plays we did together, but that would take time and for another book; however, a few of the plays did stand out. One, of course, was the play that started it all called *Visit to a Small Planet* as this was our first play we did together and a play that I will never forget. Then there was *My Three Angels,* where we played man and wife just before we got married, that was pretty funny. After all we got married right after this play, and so when you see her, you would see me, and vice versa, we became as one.

All the plays that I acted in, she did my makeup, and I was the envy of many people because I had a personal makeup artist. Ha! Now like I stated, we did a lot of plays together where I was either running lights and sound or helping building sets or even stage managing. I even codirected a play called *Guys and Dolls*. It was a lot of fun, and I hated that it all had to come to an end. But in October 1989, my contract finally ran out, and thus I had to move back to St. Louis. Lucky for me, the company put me on another contract, which kept me in St. Louis. This time I had a family to accompany me back to St. Louis, and it felt good knowing that I had someone who will love me through good times and bad times and who will always be by my side.

CHAPTER 4

The Big Move Back to St. Louis

So now it came time to move back to St. Louis. It was late October 1989, and my company wanted to wait until the very last minute before sending me home, but I told them the base was cutting out a lot of contractor's contracts because of budget cuts. My company held out to the very last minute in hopes of getting it renewed. At the end of October, there was no sign of getting a new contract, so the company finally decided to move me back to St. Louis and reassigned me to another contract back in St. Louis, and thus they gave me only two weeks to get everything ready. A lot of things had to take place before we could leave. I had to let the landlord know that I was moving, and then I began packing. Dea, of course, had to give her job a two-week notice of quitting her job because of the move as we were married, and she had to leave with me. Now that I had a family, I wound up with a lot more stuff to pack, then what I had when I first moved down to Warner Robins.

It took time to get everything pack up, plus we had to get a mover to move us. As you know, Dea had two daughters, but only one came with us as Michelle decided to stay in Warner Robins since she had lots of her friends and a boyfriend there and didn't want to leave. However, Chris decided to move back with us, and that meant only three of us were moving back to St. Louis. The good thing was the company paid for my trip back to St. Louis, and that was great as they put me on full expenses, which means that they paid for everything, mileage, food, and a motel to stay while I find a more permanent place to live in St. Louis.

The motel we stayed at had two-bedroom suites, and that was great for the three of us to stay. We got up early and began looking a for a more permanent place that would fit our needs. In looking for a place to live, I needed to find a place big enough for all our stuff and yet be close to work. We finally found a very nice place that was about two thousand square feet, a very large townhouse, and was in a good neighborhood. We signed a lease and then began to get ready for our things to arrive at our new apartment. We began to get ready to settle in our new apartment, and hopefully it would last a long time. This place was close enough to my work, and I began to work back in the shop, and things started to look good for me with my company.

Dea, on the other hand, had to find a job, and she first got a temp job downtown St. Louis and then had to drive back to our apartment, which was a little distance from what she was used too. In fact, she got lost the first day of working from downtown and then drove past our apartment, but luckily, she realized that she went too far and finally found her way home.

Chris and I almost panic at the time because we did not have cell phones like we do now a days and so we had to wait and hope she made it okay. She did manage to find her way, and as time went on, she got better at making the daily trek. Several months later, she got a more permanent job much close to our apartment, which made me feel better. After all St. Louis isn't like Warner Robins, and it's much bigger with a lot more traffic and thus a lot more dangerous.

In my new job, I began working a lot of hours, and Dea wound up working nights, but all was good. Chris went to community college and got her degree, and things were looking pretty good. So for the first year, there we had a pretty good stay and enjoyed everything. After Chris got her associate degree, she managed to get a job with Disney World and move down to Orlando in Florida as stagehand and then moved onto "Disney on ice" as a seamstress.

With one daughter out of the house, another one moved back. My daughter was having problems, and I had to make a trip to go get her from New Mexico and bring her and her husband at the time back to St. Louis so that they could start a new life. Sarah got a job and decided to move out as she found a place to live. However, that marriage didn't last, and she wound up with a wonderful new husband, and both were doing just fine. In fact, they wanted to start a new life away from St. Louis, so they moved out to Colorado Springs to live and go to college.

Now it was Michelle's turn to move back, but by this time, Dea and I decided to buy a house as our rent was getting more expensive each year. I felt that we were throwing our money away since I could not take any deductible off on the rent. I figured that since I was paying a lot of income tax that we could do a bit better buying a house. For the first time in my life, I will own a house, have a good job, have a wonderful wife, and have children that love me (even though they were up in age). Life was good.

Michelle came to live with us (it was like a revolving door with one kid going and one kid coming back, but that was okay as I enjoy all of my kids). During the time Michelle lived with us, she found a very nice guy, and they wound up getting married. It was pretty funny as the youngest daughter got married first, and the oldest daughter got married last. Ha! Shouldn't it be the other way around?

Michelle's wedding cost a pretty penny, but it was well worth it as she married a very nice guy. Now as time was moving along pretty well, things begin to change. My job got more evolve as I begin to work nights and then switch to days and was in charge of the lab on the project that I was working on. More importantly than that, technology was fast improving, and when I thought having a pager was nice, cell phone was all the raged. Of course, at this time, they didn't call them cell phone but mobile phones. At any rate, things were looking pretty good until the layoffs began.

Even though I was on contract with the project that I was working on, I still could be replaced. In fact, it came down to the fact at one point that if a certain contract didn't get approved, there were two of us that would get laid off. As fate once again stepped in, the contract was approved, and I was able to stay on with the company.

Dea herself had a change in her company name since a lot of companies where being taking over or downsized. Her company got bought out, just like mine, and yet we both managed to hang onto our jobs, but she was getting burnt out by working nights all the time. Well, you are not going to believe this, but fate has once again step in, and I had to make a big decision as to what to do next. I heard about a big contract coming up that would take me to Europe. That sounded good, but first I had to talk it over with my wife to make sure we could do it.

First, I had to find out the details as to the pay and what it meant in moving overseas; second, I had to make sure we could afford it on my salary alone, and thirdly I had to let my current boss know that I was thinking of switching jobs. I figure that since this was a five-year contract that I would be pretty safe in not getting laid off and thus maintain a good working status. Dea and I sat down, and we discussed the idea of going to Germany on a five-year contract and hopefully get out of debt and make some extra money. Plus, she probably could get a job at the army hospital as well, and we could really make a good living.

Then when we come back, we would be set, in case I couldn't get another job. I told my current boss that I wanted to transfer to the new project and even though he didn't want me to go, as I was doing a great job (job of three people, ha!) He did not stand in my way and gave me the okay of switching to the new contract and thus the move to overseas has begun. This was the best thing I could have done because of bigger layoffs that came later, and I was sure that I would have been laid off during that time.

Dea had a big choice to make, she could have stayed behind me for a couple of months as she was working for a company who was about to pay off in stocks at the beginning of the year or come with me. She chose to come with me and after my training down in West Plains for a couple of weeks we began the big move to overseas.

CHAPTER 5

An Overseas Assignment

Finally, the day came when we had to get things ready to move overseas as now, I began a new assignment and on a new project that at first was to be for only five years, but as you will see, it lasted a bit longer than that.

Before we could move there were a couple of things, we had to do before leaving. First, I had to quit my current project and switch to this new project that would take me overseas. Second, I had to go to West Plains, Missouri, to be trained on the new project so that I can be ready once I get to my assignment. Then of course, Dea had to once again quit her job in order to move with me. Since our daughter Chris had met a very nice man and was planning on getting married, they had to plan their wedding in a hurry before we left. It is nice to have all our daughters married before we left for our big adventure. We were scheduled to fly out on the fourteenth of November, and so Chris and Mike had to be married before we left, which they did on the thirteenth of November. Talk about cutting it close. Wow!

They got married in our house and had the reception in the house right after the little ceremony. Since the company would not ship any furniture, we had to put everything in storage. However, we did leave some items for Chris and her new husband Mike as they didn't have anything, and they were going to stay in our house. You see, instead of selling the house or renting it out we, gave Chris and Mike the option of staying in the house and taking care of it while we were overseas, and we would always have a home to come back to. We only put into storage what they didn't need, and I couldn't take with me. Since we could only take what was necessary, the company gave us $600 to buy furniture overseas once we find a place to live. So things got off fairly well: Chris and Mike were married on Friday November 13, and that day I had to pick up our airplane tickets to fly out on November 14 to arrive in Germany on November 15.

Friday the thirteenth is usually a sign of bad luck to some but for Chris and Mike a sign of good fortune as they were happily married for many years. Now Dea and I had our luggage pack ready to go and our holding packages were ready to be picked up as well. All I had to do was picked up the tickets on Friday from the company so that we can fly out on Saturday. Now here was a funny part, I went to my company and picked up the tickets which I thought were both our tickets but when we got to the airport, I found that the company forgot to give me Dea's ticket. She was about to panic, and I told her not to worry as I could buy a new ticket for her and then settle with the company later. We were after all on full expenses, and they knew we were going to fly together. We flew with another coworker and his family and that was fun at least we would know someone while flying as the flight would take about fourteen hours.

First, we flew into Atlanta airport and then nonstop to Frankfurt. This was our first time flying overseas but lucky we had other coworkers who were already there to meet us and drive us to where we would be living. We flew into Frankfurt, but our jobs took us to Ramstein AB, which was about ninety-plus miles south. They even set up a temp apartment for us to stay at while we look for a more permanent place. Boy not having been overseas before everything was pretty strange and yes, I didn't speak German but managed to get by during my assignment. When we got off the plane and begin to look around, we thought we went back in time as everything seem to be from a time back in the 50s. So this was very exciting and a bit scary since we had never been overseas anywhere before.

As we rode with my coworker, he discussed how things were and what to expect and what we needed to do. First of course we had to find a more permanent place to live which we did and then we had fun going out to find furniture to put in the apartment for us to live in and boy that was an experience I'll never forget. Since it was late November 1998, we didn't have much of a Christmas that year. We just had a simple getting together with our coworkers and having a good time. During this time (1998 and 1999), Germany was still using the German Frank as their money and that was great since our dollar equal two franks. However, as time went by, things change, and most of Europe went to the euro dollar, and that was reverse being that 1 euro is equal 1.40 US dollar, so things began to get very expensive. Lucky we were on full expenses and the company paid for our rent and cars and so it wasn't too bad.

Well, now that we got settled into our new home for the time being, things began to look pretty good. I was the parts manager in charge of parts for the program that I was on, and thus I had to set up a warehouse for all the parts and begin to ship them out wherever needed. While I was getting my job set up to receive and ship parts on my program, Dea decided to look for a job, but unfortunately, she could not get hired at the Army Hospital at Landstuhl. At this point, I will not get into as to why she could not get hired, but instead she worked in the arts and craft shop and later at the roller rink and then finally landing a job at the Base Exchange (BX for short). So here we were now living in Germany and far away from our family.

Now the fun began as we visited several countries and places within Germany. First, we went to Chez Republic and bought some crystal items along with a very large wooden chess set. I needed a large chessboard to be able to play with chess pieces that Chris and Dea made for me one year. The house that we lived in was actually over a small shop, which we had set up as a warehouse, but as more items got shipped, I had to not only look for bigger place to live but find a bigger place for a warehouse, which we did. Now living overseas our company would pay us one trip per year to fly back to the states which we did take each year. However, making these trips back home was a tiring effort as well, but we managed to do okay.

Now that we were settled in, we began touring many places within Germany, France, and England, as well some neighboring countries. My favorite place was the black forest, which we visited several times especially on my birthday. We also bought two grandfather clocks as well. We took a tour on our fifteenth wedding anniversary to Paris and visit the famous night club called the Moulin Rouge. That was great as we had a front row seat, and I got hit twice with the dancing girl's boa. Ha! Plus, we took a tour of Paris and then tour some of the wineries around France. That was a great tour.

We also took several tours around Germany as well, visiting several castles. During the early part of our stay in Germany, Dea managed to be able to walk around pretty well, and thus we did several shopping as well as touring some old castle. We even went to Venice in Italy, and that was a great experience. I wasn't too sure about this as we had to take a boat ride from Italy's mainland to Venice, which was basically an island. You see, Dea would easily get seasick, and being her first boat ride, she did okay. We even went on a gondola ride while there as that was the best way to see Venice. Another tour we went on was to visit a castle and had diner like they did back in the olden days, that was a lot of fun. I just wish I had taken more pictures of us during this time.

We also visit England on several occasions, but one trip, we went by Fairy, and thus again I was worried about Dea getting seasick. She did pretty good going over to England, but on the way back, well, it was a bit windy and thus a little bit wavier, but again she managed to do okay. We also visit Luxembourg and visit the site of united states graveyard where General Patton was buried. That was very interesting and informative. We also visited Bern, the capital of Switzerland, and that again was very interesting. Like I mentioned, during the early part of our stay, Dea managed to walk a lot and was able to do a lot of things, but as time went by, it became harder for her to get around, and thus, she started to slow down more and more, and our tours became less and less to the point where she could not do them anymore.

One thing was that she wound up smashing her elbow when she fell in a restaurant and thus had to have several surgeries on her elbow to get it corrected and for the elbow to heal correctly. Then she had a thyroid surgery and finally back surgery in a German hospital. I just wish she was able to do more, and we could have travelled more, but alas it wasn't meant to be.

Also, during this time, we had to move two more times, but each time to a nicer house however in Germany, there are very few ranch-style houses, which means a lot of stairs that we had to go up and down and no carpet, mostly tile or wooden floors, which made it even harder for her to get around. Now the big thing was that I was hoping to stay as long as I could before I had to go back home and retire, but since she was working for the BX and she was unable to work there any more, we lost our logistic support, and thus we would have to go on the economy.

Not being able to go to the army hospital was a big factor in the decision to go back home. I was hoping that we could at least do a couple of more tours, but fate has stepped in once again, and we had to pack up everything and move back home. Since there were no new jobs for me to go to within my company I had to retire. I was sixty-six years old and could retire anytime.

I really could not believe that we had stayed over in Germany for fifteen years, and also, we went under the German Social Security System as well. However, it was time as fate would have it, and poor Dea wasn't able to do much and having her going up and down the stairs made things worse for her. So I called up the company and got things ready, and we pack our stuff and homeward bound we went. The good news was that the company did pay for part of our stuff to be shipped home. The one thing that I wanted, and I had to ship on my own was my 2010 Jeep Wrangler, which I did. Well, it was now July 14, 2014, and we managed to fly back without too much trouble. Going home for the last time was a bittersweet ride. Oh, I made sure we went first class. However, by this time, I had made a lot of friends and loved the food and the country, and I would miss it, after all fifteen years in one place was a long time but now it was time to move back and begin a new chapter.

CHAPTER 6
The Big Move Back Home

Now comes the big move of our lives and what I had to do in order to make it happen. Living overseas for fifteen years, we had collected a lot of things like furniture, collectables, and my favorite thing, a 2010 Jeep Wrangler. But first things first. We first had to come up with a place to live back in the States. Where to live became a big question. Do we move to Belleville, Illinois, or do we stay on the other side of the river and move into our old house in St. Louis, Missouri? We talked about it for a while, but since I was going to retire, it was better to live in Illinois. We felt that the house in St. Louis was just going to be too small for us to live in. Plus, Chris and Mike were still living in the house at the time, and they needed to find a place to live as well.

For a couple of months, I looked on both side of the Mississippi, but I really could not find what I wanted in a house. I wanted a house with one acre of land and being all brick. The question becomes on where do we look to find a nice place to live that would hold all our furniture and stuff. Our son-in-law, Dwayne, had an idea of using his realtor to find us a nice house. He did, but we needed to move fast as this house wasn't going to last long on the market.

We agreed, and with the help of Dwayne, we were able to buy this house site on seen. However, Dwayne and Michelle did Skyped us, and we could see what it looked like but still had no real clue as to the real size other than what we saw via the Internet. This house did meet our basic needs of being all brick with about 3,800 square feet setting on one acre of land. This sounded good to us, and thus

I had Dwayne be our power of attorney so that he could sign the paperwork, and we would have everything in place for the big move back home.

Now that we had a house to go to, we had to figure out just what to keep and what to get rid of before the packers came to pack us. That was a big chore, and so we had to set down and just go through everything. Boy, that was tough. I could not believe just how much stuff we had collected over the years until we got ready to move. I mean we had lived in Germany for fifteen years, and over this time, we collected a lot of things. We did manage to finalize on what to take and what to leave, and it took one forty-foot trailer to pack everything.

Wow, that was a lot of stuff!

Now there was the cost of moving as well, but lucky for us, our company would pay for part of moving our stuff. This meant that for what it cost to fly first class with our holding bag full of stuff versus having it ship my entire stuff by ground. It almost came out to be about the same, but we had to pay the difference, which was okay by me as we wanted to ship all that we could back home. Now that we had a house to go to and our stuff being packed up getting ready for the move, there was a couple of more items which we had to do before we could leave. One was to ship my Jeep back to the States. Since I fell in love with my 2010 Jeep Sahara Unlimited, I wanted to ship it back home as well. However, the company doesn't pay for this, so this was totally on me.

Knowing this, I made sure I had enough money. Then of course, I had to time this just right to have it arrive back in the States at the same time that I would be back in the States to pick it up at the port. Things were looking pretty good. We had gotten a moving company to move our stuff, and I got my Jeep ready to ship back to the United States, so the only thing left was for Dea to quit her job once again and to get tickets to fly back home.

I decided that Dea and I would fly first class as a treat, and it would be easier on her since her health was declining. Funny, but I just could not believe that after fifteen years, I was going back home again for the final time and be living in a nice house. It was this new house that we bought that was the most amazing part. Once all the paperwork was completed on buying our new home and the tickets bought that we began the big trip back home. It took a couple of months, but in August of 2014, we arrived home and moved in with Michelle and Dwayne for a while until our stuff showed up. I also began my retirement since there was no jobs for me to transfer to within the company.

I could not imagine of retiring at this time, but I had enough time to retire as I had thirty-three years with my company as well as receiving Social Security since I was now sixty-six years old. Dea was already drawing social security, and with both our income, we were able to have a fairly good income. Plus, we had our retirement saving as well. We fell in love with our new house with a walkout basement and plenty of room for all our collectables and then some. We finally got all the furniture set up and got everything put into place, and by September, we were living in our new home.

Chris and Mike had found a house they could afford nearby to where my house was in St. Louis and thus moved out of our old house. We managed to get the house setup for selling; as I need to get rid of it quickly since I did not want to pay for two houses, we sold the house as is and managed to get out from that payment. At this point, the only thing left was to pick up my Jeep at the port in Georgia and drive it back to our house. Now we have a beautiful home on a nice one-acre yard where we could enjoy our retirement and enjoy being with our kids and grandchild. Life was good for a while, and we just enjoyed life and looking forward to being home again for good and not have to work for a living.

CHAPTER 7

The Final Days

W ell, here we are at home back in the USA and enjoying our new home, and it was a pretty home indeed. All was going along pretty well except that Dea was still having medical problems. She had back surgery, thyroid, and elbow surgery while overseas, and I thought I would lose her because of the amount pain she was in and that the elbow surgery had to be performed four times before it was all done. That took a lot out of her as she did wind up with infection during this time and became very weak, but she pulled through it and seemed to be doing pretty well.

Then the last surgery on her back, I think is what took the toll on her, and she wasn't able to work and really need to come home to the States since it was hard being in a German hospital and trying to understand the nurses. Then her kidney was acting up, and thus it was time. Also, at this point in time, I had a kidney stone removed, and I, too, was beginning to have some medical problems. I really didn't want to have the doctors overseas to work on me as I had a really good doctor back home, and so with all this, we really need to go home and hopefully get better and enjoy life in our brandnew home.

First, I was diagnosed as having stage 4 prostate cancer and went with chemo treatment as well as taking a shot every six months and then taking hormone pills, which I am still taking to this day. The wild part is that with stage 4 cancer, the life expectancy is one to two years, but here I am eight years later and still going strong.

Now after my chemo treatment, Dea was also having problems with her kidney, and it was found that she had kidney cancer. While we were going through all this treatment and doctor visit, both of her daughters were able to visit with us and help us get through all this treatment. They tried her on one pill only to find it was too much for her and then switched to another pill, but still it was doing more harm than good.

Life just wasn't fair. I mean, first, it was me being diagnose in October 2014 and then with her later that year. Lucky for the both of us, Dea's daughters were there to help us and stood by us while we were undergoing various treatments. I did my chemo infusion pretty well without too much trouble, just losing my hair as expected, and with taking these hormone treatment pills, I tend to get hot flashes, which the girls thought was a bit funny. Haha!

Now Dea didn't do the chemo infusion but did take chemo pills and that was very rough on her. As time went by, she began having a hard time eating, and thus it made it tough on me trying to find something for her to eat, but I did manage, and for the most part, I learned how to cook more things, plus from time to time, we ate out, which made it nice. I took her to places she loved to eat, and things were going a long fairly well, but she just kept getting run down.

With having her denture problems, it was becoming harder for her to eat, and I had to cut up the food and make sure she ate it as I really tried to keep her healthy. The pills were just too much for her with all her other problems. They look at doing surgery but felt that if they go in and remove the kidney, the cancer would spread more quickly, and then she would have more problems. The pills were the way to go, but still I wish there was something I could do or even help her in some way.

At least I took her places that she loves to go since she loves shopping, and I hoped that she was still enjoying life. I know that she really loved our new home as she mentioned it several times but as she got weaker, she could not help me any more in decorating it for the holidays, especially for Christmas.

Having to worry about me with my prostate cancer, I focused on her, helping her to the best I could, and let me tell you, being a caretaker is very tough. Again, having her daughter around was a big help. Things were, like I said, slowly going downhill, and I was at my wits end in trying to keep her healthy and yet take her places where she could enjoy going. I even bought a wheelchair to help her get around since she was getting weaker each day.

Then came the day in late 2017, when she fell and broke her shoulder bone. They could not put it in a cast but told her to keep it in a sling and try not to move it. Well, that is easier said than done, especially if you are right-handed, and it was the right shoulder that you broke. Boy, I can't tell you how many times she has fallen and needed my help in getting her up and to the doctors. I mean, while we were overseas, she was a bit heavy, but now since she wasn't eating that much. She has lost a lot of weight, and I could pick her up.

I mean that she had fallen out of bed several times, and I was able to pick her up and put her back. I tried to make her as comfortable as possible, but it was getting tough on me as well, and now with a broken shoulder bone, things began to really go downhill. Still her daughters were right there to help her and me, which made it easier on me. But still I could see that she was struggling and not knowing how or what more I could do. I just kept her as comfortable as possible and made sure she was happy.

She got so weak that we had to finally take her to the hospital and try and give her the nutrients that she desperately needed, but it was a losing battle. We did manage to spend one last Christmas at Michelle's house, but the following year was going to be the real test. She went into the hospital in early January 2018 and just kept getting weaker and weaker. Then the doctor came in and told us that she was beyond the point where her body was using more energy than what she was taking in and that wasn't a good thing.

Now we had to decide on getting her to a hospice center as it wasn't going to be much longer before she would pass. We looked around and found a very nice facility to put her in while we waited

for her last days. Her two daughters and my daughter Sarah stayed by her bed until the final days. It was January 31, 2018, that she finally breathed her last breath, and she was gone. Wow! I had really hoped that she would live as long as me, but the good Lord knew it was time, and since she was hurting and had a hard time eating and was always in pain that it was time.

 So I said my final goodbye, and I watched her take her last breath. I know that she is in a much better place. I know that she is looking down upon me and helping me through the days. However, it still hurts a lot as we became soulmates and really depended on each other, but now it was time for me to let her go and to go through it alone. I know that she was happy, but still it is hard to let go. I will now go and try and do the best I can and make her proud by keeping up with my writings and just be with her daughters and helping them out as best I can along with my daughter. I know that even though she is gone physically, she will always be within my heart and will always be in my memories. May she always rest in peace and know that someday I will be with her, and we can be together forever again.

ABOUT THE AUTHOR

Patrick was born and raised in Michigan until his family moved out west in 1968 where he attended New Mexico Tech college. He later dropped out of college to join the US Air Force during the Vietnam war in 1971. While in the air force, he managed to get a BS degree in electronic engineering and technology with an AS in computer science. After nine and a half years with the air force, he was honorably discharged in 1980 and went immediately to work for a company in St. Louis and later met his wife. He managed to get his MS degree in management and began to do a lot of traveling together with his wife. His wife was his inspiration, and he started writing poetry to which several of them got published. It was his wife who inspired him to go beyond poetry to writing a book. Patrick retired in 2014, and with a lot of time off, he was once again inspired by his wife to begin the journey of writing a book about the life they had.